Stories Along The Way

Stories Along The Way

Paula E. Gelbach

Illustrator

Kathleen K. Potts

Library of Congress Control Number:		2013913081
ISBN:	Hardcover	978-1-4836-7187-1
	Softcover	978-1-4836-7186-4
	Ebook	978-1-4836-7188-8

This book was printed in the United States of America.

Rev. date: 08/22/2013

To order additional copies of this book, contact:
Xlibris LLC
1-888-795-4274
www.Xlibris.com
Orders@Xlibris.com
133792

Dedication

I dedicate this book to Scott Johnson, my long-time dependable computer teacher without whom it is questionable if my manuscripts would ever get to their destination(s) correctly and on time. In addition, I want to give special mention to my husband, Charles, who gave me the needed support and the encouragement to accomplish my tasks. My husband was with me when most of these true stories took place.

Contents

Chipmunk's Surprise

Living in Maine in the winter means that dealing with rodents is likely to become a part of life. Not like a relative, nor a friend, but someone or something that moves into your space uninvited. It lives in the garage, in the barn, and yes even in the house. It might be a chipmunk, squirrel or something we never would have thought of wanting to move in with us, who comes and likes to hang around.

Returning to Maine one year after spending several winter months in Florida, we had a surprise. We had left our second car in our garage while we were gone. Before we left we thought we had "rodent proofed" our car per the instructions of a native Mainer. We were told that all sorts of dire things happen if a rodent makes a home in your car, among them chewed wires. So, following the instructions of the garage manager, we stuffed steel wool into the exhaust pipe and all openings in the car. We were assured that neither mice, squirrels nor chipmunks could navigate the twisted material to get into the car.

Confident that all was well with our car when we returned home, we removed the steel wool and drove to the post office to pick up the mail. My husband went into the post office and I remained in the car. All of a sudden smoke was streaming fast and furiously out from under the hood. My husband came running. He looked under the hood, smelled a horrible smell and felt the heat. He drove the car very fast, to the one and only car wash for miles, while smoke continued to billow fast and furiously from under the hood. Cars coming toward us swerved to get out of our way.

The first thing the car wash operator did was empty his trash cans so that if he had to put burning material into the can it would not ignite the things already there and cause more fire. The car wash operator vacuumed out the smoldering fire under the hood. Then we all held our noses and took a look. The air cleaner, the round shape sitting on top of the engine, was filled with acorns and pine needles. The heat from the engine had started the acorns and all the debris smoldering.

We never did learn how to effectively rodent-proof our car the years we lived in Maine. But we did learn of chipmunk surprises.

Creative Cooking

I don't mind cooking. It is the deciding what to cook that sometimes buffalos me (buffalo/ bison is good eating). The world needs a new edible animal that sits between fish and chicken in the meat case at the supermarket. I don't mean a big animal. In any event it wouldn't sit in its entirety proudly upright between the fish and chicken. It would mimic chicken in that it would be prepared by the butcher into different cuts readily identifiable, if possible.

I have often thought that the reason there are so many cookbooks in libraries and bookstores as well as self-proclaimed gourmet cooks is that everyone who takes on chef duties has to figure out ways to make the old stand-bys taste and look exciting on the plate or fit into special diet guidelines. Now a new animal could do that all by itself just by being a new food and it would transform some cooks from just being creative into gourmets.

My husband's family had three categories of cooking or baking that they didn't know they had, but I recognized them right away. One category was, "this is delicious". Another category was "this tastes very good". The third category, when asked how the particular food was enjoyed, the answer was, "this is very different" or "it'll eat". I really didn't like the expression "it'll eat" so very much since my cooking often fell in that category. So whether it was true or not I translated in my head "it'll eat" into "creative". If my in-laws were alive today I think they would say I finally graduated to the "tastes very good" category but as a newlywed the things I made sometimes were indeed creatively different, falling into the "it'll eat" category.

As a newlywed I discovered rubber gelatin one day when I used a large gelatin package with half the amount of required water. It gives the gelatin a new consistency and intense flavor. The top-crust pumpkin pie I made "from scratch" was the way I thought I had seen my mother-in-law make pumpkin pie. In truth she liked to use fresh pumpkin and cream in her recipe but no top crust. The three-layer spice birthday cake with caramel icing is my husband's favorite cake and my mother-in-law made it for him each year on his birthday. She probably made it other times as well but definitely on my husband's birthday.

Because at that time I was still newly married and a different sort of creative baker I had to think what to do with cake batter enough for three separate layers and only one cake pan. Suddenly inspiration hit and I put all the batter in a Dutch oven to bake. In my case a Dutch oven was a very large and deep casserole type dish. The result was in a fourth category not deserving of a name. The category was not "it'll eat", because it wouldn't.

The best tasting caramel icing (according to my husband) was also made by his mother. With my mother-in-law's recipe we had to move quickly and ice the cake before the icing hardened. We had two young children at the time of this creative venture, and why I invited our young children to help I'll never know. Mothers do this sort of thing I have discovered. Suffice it to say that we sang "Happy Birthday" that year while standing around a birthday cake with a large lump of icing right in the middle of the top layer of the cake which had sunk to the bottom layer. It was a creative cake. My husband said "it'll eat". And it did.

Poor Judgment

Poor judgment does not always lead to a perilous situation. Everyone uses poor judgment now and again and it might result in our embarrassment, but not necessarily in our peril. My poor judgment put me in a perilous situation at the age of 15 that was both embarrassing and I considered life threatening to my "successful" Jr. High School years.

Three other girls and myself were close friends in school and liked to do things together. Most things had to be done before school, after lunch, or after school (if we arranged it ahead of time). We lived far from one another even though we attended the same school. There were no school buses. All of us took trolleys and city buses and then walked a distance to our homes. If we stayed after school to play tennis, for example, it would get late and parents had to agree to come and drive us home.

We were not all in the same classes at the same time, but all of us certainly liked gym. At that time there were few "tumbling" activities. Exercises had not yet come into their own as "fitness," and more of the games such as basketball, soccer, archery and golf were played. Of the two gym teachers, one was extremely nice and the other made it a bit of a challenge to gain her favor.

After lunch one day, the four of us had extra time and we decided to go to the gym because sometimes it was left open for activities after lunch. We wanted to play ping pong. When we got to the gym the paddles and balls were behind a locked window and no gym teacher was in sight to get them for us. We decided to raise the next window, which was not locked, and reach over and get the equipment. At that very moment the least liked gym teacher appeared from the back room where her office was located. We ran. After a minute we caught our breath and decided to go back to the gym and apologize to the gym teacher and explain what we were doing. Good judgment finally raised its head.

The gym teacher did not accept our apology and reported us to the Vice Principal with the recommendation that all four of us be expelled from the Honor Society. Now poor judgment turned into a perilous situation because Honor Society members were looked up to and if someone was expelled that was really terrible. However, our homeroom teacher and the nice gym teacher saw a case of poor judgment, not criminal activity, and defended us.

After we had apologized once again, and the Vice Principal talked with us about using good judgment, we were forgiven and not expelled from the Honor Society. The peril was averted but all four of us never ever forgot that incident. We didn't talk about it much, but we never forgot it.

Two Big Black Boots

One winter, just before Christmas, my husband and I took time out from our busy lives to attend our friends' Holiday Party. They had built a new home and they wanted us to see it and wish them well. As we climbed the front steps, I tripped on the top step. I was in pain, but I limped along saying nothing that would interfere with the good time everyone was having.

Home again, when the pain only got worse, my husband insisted on taking me to the emergency room at the hospital. The doctor on duty diagnosed a broken left ankle. Since it was not out of alignment, the prescription was a big black boot, otherwise known as a brace. My foot slipped into it. There were shoe laces from the top of my foot to my knee that had to be laced and then tied. Then velcro straps were put on top of the laces to cause more tightening.

We traveled to Florida a week later, for a winter break that we had planned some time before my accident. Several days after we established ourselves and unpacked, I fell again and this time broke my right ankle. It turned out to be a stress fracture. Once again the break was "clean" and in alignment so the doctor prescribed a boot (brace) for my right foot. It too had laces all the way up to my knee covered over by four or five Velcro straps that were to keep the boot snug and tight. Now I had matching footwear. Somehow knowing that both feet matched did absolutely nothing to make me feel better. Nor did it make me feel better when my friends teasingly called the boots fashionable.

Both doctors, the one in Maine and the one in Florida wanted me to wear these boots all the time, and to bed at night at least for two weeks. The whole process of healing took almost all the several months we were in Florida. I did come home without my big black boots but by then the doctor had exchanged them for a matched pair of little black boots.

I am sure you know that velcro sticks to everything. The velcro just loved my pajamas. As I freed one place, the boot caught on another. I finally got the "hang of it" and climbed into bed. Then began the tussle of trying to free one boot from the blanket without getting the velcro from the other boot caught in the blanket instead. I wrestled back and forth, from one leg to the other leg with all my strength and I still did not have both legs free at the same time. As I lay there thinking I would be awake all night, I realized help was in the next room. “Honey, I need help, I’m stuck,” I hollered. My husband came and the first thing he said was, “What have you been doing? The bed is all torn up.” I gave him a look that I thought professional wrestlers would give their opponent when wrestling. He said no more. He just got busy untangling me.

I don’t know if it was the wrestling look or not, but my husband tried cheerfully to accomplish this task of untangling me for the next two weeks.

Imagination Rises With The Sun

I have always had a problem with my laughter. Kids at school would whisper, “What are you laughing at?” Now, laughter in and of itself is not a problem, but not being able to stop, or when sharing what I am laughing at and no one else joins in, therein lies the problem. I am sure people who notice me hiding my face think I have lost my mind. I often have the ability to see the funny side of things or make up in my mind a “funny side.”

Please note, I do not see the funny side of earthquakes, tornadoes, hurricanes, floods or other real disasters. Nor do I laugh at other people and their predicaments. I usually begin with something funny I did and then imagine it in a much different situation or bigger scene.

One Easter Sunday, my husband and I attended Easter Sunrise Service at our church. As always it was held outside on the church grounds. In preparation, the staff had set about 50 metal folding chairs in rows facing the pastor. As the service got underway and I sat there listening, I felt myself begin to sink. The ground was extremely wet and my husband noticed that there were no "feet" on the bottoms of the legs of my chair. The metal legs just cut right through the soggy, wet soil. I was going down, down, down. It was a strange feeling and because I was holding my laughter inside, it made me weak and I could not get myself up and out of that sinking chair.

My husband rescued me. There began a minor shuffling around and other people who saw what happened were beginning to check the feet on the legs of their own chairs. My husband got me another chair with the proper feet. And trying not to make any more disturbance I sat down once more.

Then a giggle attack struck me. I was imagining the pastor looking out at the people sitting in front of him, and one by one his listeners' chairs would sink down into the soggy soil. One by one each person would almost disappear. At least they seemed to be sitting much lower than they were when they first sat down. I even went so far as to imagine the pastor wondering why he was shaking so few hands at the end of the service when he knew for a fact he had seen many more people sitting in front of him in the service that day.

Well, I did finally get a grip on myself, and after the service, as the sun was rising, my husband, not knowing what my imagination was up to, said to me, “I’m glad you thought it was funny. You could have been hurt.”

A potential tragedy was averted and thank goodness the hazard only became one in my mind. Riding home I imagined again lots of folks in the congregation outside that morning sinking and that is why the pastor had fewer hands to shake. In my imagination I figured the pastor could have had a mystery to solve and I was the only one with the answer.

Lady Lost

I get lost easily. You might have seen me or someone like me driving down a street, looking up at a street sign on a corner trying to decide if this is where I turn or need to turn around. These are the folks that get angry stares from the people in cars passing by. I have very little sense of direction and until time passes and I learn my way, I get lost.

Imagine my chagrin when our younger daughter was about 10 years old and my husband said to me to remember to take her with me in the car when I was going someplace new so I wouldn't get lost. You see, she has an excellent sense of direction and you only have to take her to a place once and she seems never to forget how to get there even if years have gone by. This is a wonderful gift some people have.

One summer evening after dinner I noticed a sale on scarves at a department store advertised in the newspaper. I needed a scarf and since this was the last day of the sale, my husband said he would take me to the store because he had some shopping to do at a place which was across from the mall. Since we were going to almost the same place just a different store, there was no need for me to drive my own car.

I got out of my husband's car at the door of the department store closest to the scarves. We agreed that I was to come out the same door and sit on the bench outside when I was finished and he would look for me there. I bought my scarf in record time and then wandered around and took the escalator up to the main floor of the store where, to my surprise, I found another display of scarves. When I figured my husband would be outside waiting for me, I went out the door where the scarves were and waited on the bench as I was instructed. I waited and waited and waited. I waited until it began to get dark. I waited as the clerks began leaving the store one by one or in groups, chatting away. I waited as buses pulled up and stopped to take on clerks and shoppers to travel home.

It was all very interesting watching all those people. I was warm enough since it was summer and I was sitting on a comfortable bench. I wasn't unhappy. I might mention that there were no cell phones handy at the time. After some time I was beginning to get a bit concerned. I had been waiting for my husband for an awfully long time. Where was he? If he didn't come soon I was sure I would need to go for help.

All of a sudden I saw the car coming up the incline from the lower level. My husband had a relieved look on his face when he saw me. He had been searching in and out of the store all that time on the lower level of the store where I should have been. I had come out the door on the main level of the store, which had a display of scarves as well. I had lost my sense of direction and was waiting at the wrong door outside the wrong level of the store sitting on the wrong bench. My husband held his temper and so it was a quiet ride home.

Intruder in the Night

My father was away overnight at a conference when we had a rather disturbing episode. I was about 14 years old and my sister 4. After I was sound asleep one night, I felt my mother shake me awake and tell me in hushed tones that there was an intruder in the house and that I should go into my sister's room and wait there.

Her door had a lock on it. My sister and I thought the intruder had a gun and was shooting it because every so often what sounded to us like a shot rang out.

While I was waiting with my sister behind a locked door, my mother telephoned our neighbor. She knew he'd still be up. My mother said later that telephoning the police never really entered her mind. Mother unlocked the front door for our neighbor when she saw him coming up the front walkway. He carried a huge thick piece of lumber that resembled a baseball bat.

After a whispered conversation with my mother, the neighbor heard the explosion sound himself. He bolted into our kitchen followed closely by my Mother. What they saw was a dozen or so exploded hardboiled eggs sticking on the ceiling above the stove. Mother had put the eggs on to hard boil and promptly forgot all about them. All the water had evaporated and the eggs got too hot and exploded.

My mother was extremely embarrassed. My sister and I still were not sure what to make of it all and really found it a bit funny to see all those exploded eggs on our kitchen ceiling. We heard our mother apologizing and thanking our neighbor.

The real disaster adverted here is obvious. Much more damage than a burned pan and a dozen ruined eggs could have been the result.

A Love For Winston

At college, our older daughter adopted a cat she named Winston. She loved Winston, but in some ways Winston was not very lovable.

Winston was a beautiful looking cat with a shiny short gray coat and big gray eyes. His pink nose would take a prize in any pink nose contest. And he was HUGE. He liked my daughter but she got hissed at many times too, along with the rest of us. He loved to scare the life out of everybody. No one tried to pick him up without putting on leather gloves first and trying to keep him from reaching any human part. We tried to have patience with him because we all felt he had been mistreated at some point before he belonged to my daughter.

Sarah kept the cat in her dorm room in college and when she graduated she kept him with her in her apartment. When she married she kept him with her in her home. Eventually two sons were added to the household. The boys were about 6 and 8 years old when Winston finally left the household in peace.. All his life he was known as the attack cat. He hissed, clawed, scared us and occasionally drew blood. He gave Sarah's husband problems as well. I referred to Andrew as a saint as far as tolerating Winston was concerned.

The perils Winston caused, when he was around, were several and I was the one who had the most to bear since I was the one home all day. The problem was under the category of terrorizing. People wore leather coats or something heavy at times when we never quite knew where Winston was. If he landed on us from on top of the refrigerator, his claws dug into exposed flesh. And then there were the never ending times we would walk past the kitchen door and a paw would come out and swipe at us. I never went into the kitchen without fear in my heart that a swipe would come my way, and several times it did. But I always seemed none the worse for wear except a rapid heartbeat. Winston usually would give us a warning. He had the loudest hiss one could imagine.

Of course, if we were having company or I decided that day not to live in peril, I penned him in the small bathroom on the first floor for a few hours. Picking him up and putting him in that bathroom took a lot of courage. And then just as soon as the bathroom door closed behind him, he began scratching at the door.

Some folks would say we were crazy to put up with Winston's behavior. But you know what? In spite of everything, the swipes aimed at us and my talks with our daughter as to why she kept that cat and reminders to her of the peril he presented, our daughter was loyal to Winston. Our daughter loved Winston and we loved our daughter.

Kathleen K. Potts

Illustrator

Born and raised in Pittsburgh, Pa, Kathy went on to attend four years of study at Wilson College in Chambersburg, Pa. Kathy is married and the parent of four children, one with special needs. Kathy taught school for eighteen years, created puppet shows for grade school childdren about special needs children. Kathy began to paint and draw in retirement and this is the second book she has illustrated.

She currently lives in West Chester, PA.

www.ingramcontent.com/pod-product-compliance
Ingram Content Group UK Ltd.
Pitfield, Milton Keynes, MK11 3LW, UK
UKHW041833200726
13854UKWH00003BA/1118

9 781483 671864